Postcards to Shirlaine
Excerpts from a Love Story

by
R.E.B.

© 2015. All rights reserved. No part of this work may be scanned, copied, uploaded or reproduced in any form or by any means, graphically, electronically or mechanically, without written permission from the copyright holder.

First Edition
June 12, 2015

ISBN: 978-1-943492-01-5 (hard back)
ISBN: 978-1-943492-02-2 (soft cover)

*Front cover painting by Shirlaine, given to the author on their wedding day.
Egg tempera and gold leaf. 14.6 cm x 20.6 cm*

Photograph of Shirlaine, 1970, taken by the author.

*A portion of the author's royalties from the sales of this book
is to be donated to charitable organizations.*

WWW.ELMGROVEPUBLISHING.COM

For you. Forever.

Shirlaine brought beauty, magic, wonder, and more into my life. All I could offer her in return were words.

Most of the verse that I gave to her during her lifetime has been lost. Those included here are fragments, recovered from the wreckage of our life after I lost her to cancer. In my grief I continue writing to her, and that is most of what you will read.

The verse from our courtship is that of a callow youth, structured and emulating my favorite poet. If you can get through that, the rest should be easy.

Though intensely personal, a few friends and family urged me to let my verse be published because in some ways it expresses moments in their lives too. I was reluctant at first, but agreed in the hope that it may comfort those mourning a loved one by helping them see that anguish and confusion are normal and human, and that grief is not an illness to be cured or an injury to be healed, but an expression of enduring love.

I doubt there is anything new here. The sentiments are as old as love and loss, and the writing, I suspect, unremarkable. These are, in the end, just words.

R.E.B.

I. Courtship

II. Marriage

III. Grief

I. Courtship

voice drones on
until my head is beating
and my heart is crying
out
   - I love you

replies
   - Thank you
changes subject

listen!
is the heart deaf
which once was may?
the lips which once
blossomed forth life
cannot have wilted
within a single day

Courtship

the happiness found
my two years with you
lies immeasurably
beyond all

what man or god
can count on his
heaven of stars
the days of life
and love shared
twice from fall to
spring

a smile
a kiss
a tear
two hands tightly clasped
but more than this
one finds
as one
two hearts
two minds

wherever
there is a moon
a valley shrouded
in mist
a shore and a sea
a heaven above
there are we

make it
a good summer
shirlaine

summer
time of waiting watching
someones
from somewhere
bound nowhere
no ones

going always without
passion or feeling
eyes staring
without seeing

nights alone
to dream the dream
we
waking ever
to live the nightmare
i

summer
time of watching waiting
now lost, some
-how forgotten
in the upward
smiling eyes and lips
whispering

    welcome home

Courtship

perhaps I shall never know
the mystery of your eyes
the miracle by which they bear my soul
far beyond mere worlds and skies

their smallest gesture
will myself unfold, gently
as some tiniest flower
touched by the sun's rays

and if one day your heart does
wish to again fold me,
life and I will close
softly, quietly

> when your eyes (young and warm) sing
> their voice is deeper than any spring

night. dark clouds hang above
watching an invisible hand
calling down their love
to fall upon the sea and land

the winds blow along the street below
turn the corner and steal away
on tiny feet, on and on they go
rushing toward a fresh new day

a thousand fingers tap on the glass
carried by the breath of the wind this
night these magical tears pass
and touch the ground with a kiss

    nothing on earth, not even the rains
    can say what your smile so simply explains

Courtship

footsteps echo in the dark
along the street
desolate and despairing
as if ashamed the moon
hides her face
(perhaps she too is leaving)
    star light, star bright
    first star i see tonight

each breath repulsive
with the stench of self
each face i come
to along the path
sneers and says
"why are you alone?"
    i wish i may, i wish i might
    have the wish i wish tonight

people are laughing
i climb the lonely stair
lit by a dirty yellow lamp
and enter my prison
to fall upon the bed
shivering, cold, damp
    sleep, rest; prepare to meet
    tomorrow: the bitter and the sweet

judge me not too harshly
if i have in my imperfectness
wronged these deeper than
to hope mirrors which are
your eyes, if my song has
failed to capture the mystery
and magic of your every
smile and the gentle way
you have of being yourself

  my love was placed
around you to keep
  you from all unhappiness
not to be a prison

you whose fate is to grow and create
you whose very aliveness has
shown spring the way into
the waste of my soul

if another should hear
your eyes singing as they
have sung life into me
if he should find the warmth
of your kiss as i have found
and if the fingers of your soul
should touch his heart as
mine is so firmly held now
  go to his side
  without turning back

if another can give you
more than merely me
(tho you hold in your
small hands my soul)
then to you both i wish
all joy and happiness
  and (without a tear) then
  let me go, once gone
  never to return

come, enter with me

these enchanted lands
conceived in love's own womb
and born by the soul's firm hands

this world has been paid for
tenfold with Life's blood and tears;
to give will open the door

to happiness, to keep will close
us forever in our prison

Love's kingdom lies beyond the mind
only the Moon can understand
the completeness of what we find

on the other side of self when
the door is opened. give me your
hand and we shall go then

stopping only to touch every star

Courtship

the spirit of youth is broken

crumbling are hopes and dreams
the child's faith is all but forgotten
and your every glance seems

to foretell the coming of life's autumn season
where visions tumble like leaves from trees
and are trampled upon without reason

still ahead lies the winter
to cloak all in passionless cold

then shall to know become to guess
understanding turn to fear, seeing be
merely to look, and death the only yes

yet when all is lost, my love,
still shall i keep one dream:
not of once upon a time, but of

(you and me) spring

II. Marriage

Though seldom said
with life so harried,
I love you far more
than when we married.

Not long ago you caught me
watching you, as I often do.
Asked what I was doing,
I replied,
Looking at the gal I married.

There's a lot more of me,
you joked, yet I agree –
more wisdom, more strength,
more experience in life,
more of a woman, more of a wife.

More of that special spark
that first drew me to you,
and I'm still looking forward
to even more of you.

It is said that for each of us
   there is another,
and now I know it's true,
I am thankful that I found her,
and I rejoice that she is you.

Marriage

I have heard you marvel
at our good fortune
in having such wonderful
people for children.

Yet it is no mystery to me.
You see, I know the woman
who for a time put aside
her own life to help them
become who they are.

I went to sleep one night
with a young girl,
unsure and hesitant,
seeking to find her way.

I awoke to find
a woman in my bed,
strong and confident,
and together we welcomed
a bright new day.

Marriage

Gone is the young romantic
    who took you as his wife.

I know your selfish side too well
my love, and once I thought that hell
itself might be a peaceful refuge
from this thing called marriage.

The day I gave up all my dreams
    so you could play at life

I did so not out of naivety
nor high ideals, nor loyalty,
but because, knowing you even as I do,
I long ago chose love, and each new day
choose you.

On our Wedding Day

I promised to love you forever,
but that was before I learned
how long forever could become,

I said I would stay with you
through the best and the worst,
but that was before I wandered
the depths of despair alone,

I agreed to stand back and
give you room to grow,
but that was before I saw
how far away this would take you.

Thirty-three years later

Even in the stark light
of life's experience,

I know we can walk our own paths
yet do it hand in hand,

I love who you were, who you are,
and who you are becoming,

And as for my promise of long ago,
forever is far too short a time.

Marriage

No puppy love for this old dog.

I wouldn't trade you, dear mate,
for all the young bitches in heat.

You still get me howling at the moon.

III. Grief

I found my poems to you hidden in your drawer,
secretly saved by you since Christmas 1964.
My heart smeared across paper, across time.
Oh how I loved you, and love you still.

Grief

In the debris of your life I chanced upon a program,
S. Hurok presents the Bolshoi Ballet, 1962,
Marina Kondratieva and Nicolai Fadeyechev in Giselle,
your souvenir of the night when, in a borrowed car
I, awkward, frightened even, in my absurd blue suit
somehow found the courage to say, *I think I love you.*
And you, beautiful, sexy in your pink satin gown,
made my world complete with, *I think I love you too.*

Our life together was everything
we dreamed of when we found each other:
seeing this beautiful world hand-in-hand,
a chance to make a small difference in it,
wonderful children to share it with,
and a love to last forever.
We wrote our own story,
all except the happy ending.

Grief

You were so right to worry about me.
I know I promised you I wouldn't,
but I can see how easy it would be
to give up and die of a broken heart.
All I really want is to be with you.

Going through your clothes
is harder than I imagined.
Things you sewed and knitted.
The hat you were wearing
on the morning you left us.
You were so elegant
even in your tee shirts.
I know keeping your things
won't bring you back,
but it is so hard to let go.
Everything I see and touch
reminds me of you,
and it is the memories
that I most want to keep.

Grief

Thinking of you over
Vietnamese espresso
with fresh *dan tat*.
Friends who were
coming over didn't
so I'm having it by myself
and between you and me
it tastes just as good,
though I'm troubled that
I'm already getting used
to living alone.

I know I shouldn't
talk to your picture
but it is how I say good night,
how I say good morning,
how I keep you close
in the chaos
that is my life.

Grief

Two hours over a bottle
of rice whiskey to see
if I can go ten minutes
without thinking of you.
One of my most
spectacular failures.

Eight months ago I lost you forever.
You'd think something would have
changed in all that time but I still
call out your name in the dark,
cry at the most awkward times,
ask questions that have no answer.
Oh Shirlaine, my beautiful sweet Shirlaine,
you still had so much to give the world.

Grief

Going through your art I find
your quiet self-assured sensibility
far beyond the loud insecure crowd
clamoring for attention and acclaim.
Praise had little meaning for you.
Your joy was never in the result,
it was in the act of creating beauty.

I see you in our children, I feel you in the depth of my being.
You are so much a part of me that
I no longer know where I end and you begin.
Why then is there such pain in living without you?

Grief

Having known paradise with you,
I know something of hell.
It is spending eternity without you.

I'm dining where you chose to come
the last time we were able to take you out.
It was a struggle for you in the wheel chair,
you ate so slowly but relished every bite.
You had such strength and courage
even when life was an epic struggle for you,
even when you knew it would only get worse.
How I wish I had even a little of your courage
to live what's left of my life without you.

Grief

Going through your shoes and handbags
I compliment myself for not losing it
until I find one of your old tops
on the floor in the back of the closet.
Simple, quilted, warm, the red one
that you like to wear at Christmas.
I sit on the bed hugging it,
crying like the day you left me.

I know that we have no control over life.
I know that when our time is up, it is up.
I know that death takes those who deserve to live.
I know that together we lived the life we wanted.
I know I had more happiness any mortal can expect.
I know we had a love that many only dream of.
I know I am the luckiest man in the world.
I know all of this and so much more.
But knowing does nothing to console a broken heart.

Grief

Listening to a friend complaining
about shopping with his wife,
I can only bite my tongue,
not telling him how I would
sell my very soul for the chance
to shop one more time with you.

I can't smell you,
not in your clothes,
not on your pillow,
not anywhere.
I lose more of you
every day.

Grief

I went to the ophthalmologist today,
the last of three doctors I have seen
in as many weeks as I try
to put my life back together.
Taking care of you I neglected
to take care of myself, and
like the yard we both neglected
I am overgrown and going to seed.

*Last night I drifted off to sleep
wondering if I could ever fall
in love again, so I think it not
by chance that you picked this
morning to visit me. In my
dream we were young again, not
even 20, but we remembered our
lifetime together and your awful
journey with cancer. So happy to
find each other again, we were
ready to throw away everything
and just run off together hoping
for a second chance at forever.*

Grief

Sunday afternoon, dog-tired I lie down for a nap.
We are in the mountains on a road trip and it is raining.
Rugged, beautiful, we have been here before in my dreams.
We stop in a familiar town, walk through the shops
and ask of the weather and the conditions along
the rutted back road where we plan to camp tonight.
You reach up to me, we embrace and kiss, and
like Sleeping Beauty the longed-for touch of your
eager lips breaks my slumber.
Unlike her, I could be happy lost in my dream forever.

I promised you I'd keep on going.
My head knows just what to do,
but my heart won't move ahead
if it means leaving you behind.

Grief

Now what? I made it
through another day
and the hard part
begins anew.
The part where, alone
in this empty house,
I can't avoid the truth.

I promised you I would go on living no matter what,
but finding my way in this new world isn't easy.
Today, going through old photos, I realized
I haven't lost the past, it is ever with me.
And as bleak as it seems without you in it,
I haven't lost the future, I wake in it each day.
I miss you with every breath I take,
but your life and love abide in me,
your courage is mine, and I go on.

I know why spouses often die
one after the other.
It is so tempting to give up.

Every day my heart says,
I can't live without you.
Every night my heart cries,
All I want is to be with you.
Every morning I open my eyes
to find that I am still here.

This is the best-kept secret
of the human heart:
It can somehow hold fast
to the deepest sorrow
yet allow in just enough joy
to keep a flicker of hope alive.

I look at photos of our last big trip together.
Many are photos that you took, memories
you wanted to keep even though you knew
that you had only months to live.
You were as beautiful as I have ever seen you,
yet so worried about how you might look
that you rarely let me take photos of you,
and when you did let me you seldom smiled,
so I keep my dearest memories of
that special time with you in my heart.

I made the mistake of watching
The Joy Luck Club.

Memories came flooding back
with emotions fast on their tail.
Nobody who knows you would believe
the self-doubts and insecurities
of the characters were once yours,
but I watched you tame your demons.

Part way through the film I realized
I wasn't watching as an outsider,
and marveled at life's unexpected path.
How, without realizing it, I acquired
your Chinese-American sensibilities,
and how surprised I was when you left
that they didn't leave with you,

I realized how I have changed lately.
I am now the one with the self-doubts,
wondering how it was possible that
you could have fallen in love with me,
standing here small, alone, naked,
with only my bag full of regrets
over what I could have done differently
to make your life easier, happier.

Still feeling too much of what has been lost
to let the sweetness of what we had
back into my life.

I am re-living the worst day of my life.
Even though it was a year ago
it seems like yesterday,
every detail seared into my heart.

How you, the strongest, most courageous person
I ever knew, could no longer hold up your head.
How you were still in there fighting
but your body refused to cooperate.

How people somehow knew this was the end.
How Aimée came before work,
how Tue Nam and Brenda came to say goodbye
and tell you how much they loved you.

How later in the day you just stared into space,
unable to speak, and how when Matt phoned
your eyes lit up and your mouth moved
but the words wouldn't come out.

How, alone with you for a time, I again
tried to tell you everything that was
in my heart, knowing you could hear me,
and knowing I could never say it all.

How in the night you moaned in pain,
so I gave you your morphine and
told you to hang on a little longer,
Matt would be here in the morning.

How I went to bed knowing that
you would be here when Matt came,
and how at four a.m. our helper woke me
to tell me that you were gone.

Grief

How you wanted to spend your last night
with me in our bed, and how impossible it was.
How I wanted to be at your side when you left,
but was in our bed asleep, leaving you so alone.

How I phoned Aimée, how she came over
and we sat with you until Matt came,
then the forever of silence waiting for the
hospice and funeral home people.

How our love that would last forever,
that we were once so arrogant as to think
could protect us from all comers,
was so casually brushed aside by life.

How knowing death is coming
makes it no easier when he comes,
how you were here with us one moment
then in an instant gone forever.

How I climbed into your hospital bed
to lie with my arms around you one last time,
as if that could make up for me not being there,
could make up for my letting you die so alone.

How the Hospice nurse pronounced you dead.
How they put you in a bag and took you away.
How the love of my life was taken from our home
with such cold, bureaucratic efficiency.

How, even though I knew in my heart that
what they took away wasn't really you anymore,
it still broke my heart to think of you lying
in the funeral home so alone. So alone.

Our road trips always began
with smiles at what unknown
adventure might await us.
Not so today.
Tripped up early by a song
I can't regain my balance.
Around every bend,
over every rise,
are memories of you.

Grief

Endless parade of ugly little cars
    We were made for the road, you and I,
jousting with impotent little men
    lovers, forever young, laughing, carefree
in monster SUVs
    as we made the world our own
cursing the very big rigs
    one mile at a time.
that bring the world to their door.
    Your empty seat and bunk now filled
I drive on, never reaching my goal
    with echoes of endless happy days
of driving thirty minutes
    and untold nights of love.
without tears.

Even eating up 80 miles
every hour there is still
too much time to think.
To remember driving
this same road with you,
carefree and laughing.
To take the full measure
of all that has been lost.

Grief

By now Mikey* expects
my unexpected outbursts,
my anguished cries,
my shouting your name.
With understanding eyes
he licks me as if to say
It's OK. Let it out.

Mikey is the author's Rat Terrier

These long days behind the wheel
all I can think of is how miserably
I failed at the most important task
that was ever given to me in life.
Overwhelmed trying to stay on top of
the ever immediate what when where
cooking arranging visits cleaning
chemo radiation clinical trials
meds without end amen amen,
I neglected your emotional needs.
How can I ask you to forgive me
when I cannot forgive myself?

Grief

A brutal year for poppies too.
Where once we sat in endless
fields of gold, there is only brown.
An errant poppy on the roadside
whispers as I pass that even on
the bleakest path there is hope.

I drive by my childhood
home for the last time.
Memories swirl around me
but I am a stranger here.
You can't go home again
because it isn't home anymore.
Home is where the heart is
and you have taken mine
so very far away.

Grief

Start my day in tears,
spend my day in tears,
end my day in tears.
Tears of joy
for all we had.
Tears of sorrow
for all we had.

Morning coffee in the desert takes me back
to lazy mornings with you in Saigon,
perfect cups of coffee and fresh baguettes.
To coffee beans drying in front yards
and on the roads leading to *Buôn Ma Thuôt*.
The glint of the sun off my cup
sends me back to California,
alone and desolate as her desert,
our sweet life together just out of reach.

Grief

The wildflowers here are all but finished.
When I left home your cymbidiums
were finished for the year too, all save one,
a perfect spike on the orchid that I gave you
on the day that we had been married half my life.

Alone where the Colorado Desert meets the Mojave
I can no longer contain my heartache,
screaming to everything and to nothing,
Oh Shirlaine Shirlaine Shirlaine

Grief

Children of the West, we two,
at home in these wild, lonely spaces,
self-sufficient, independent,
unafraid of life or of living.
Each of us with our own failings
yet what one of us lacks
the other has in abundance.
Together we are perfect. Perfect!
How then do I answer the call
of the coyote without you?

Hiking as we used to do, just to see what is around the bend,
I look up somehow expecting to see you in front of me.
I hear only one set of footsteps, the sound of my new life.

Grief

Where once we were greeted by wildflowers
I find only parched earth and unrelenting sun.
Where we walked with playful banter, laughter even,
there is only the sound of my boots and labored breath.
I meet a stranger and we speak of wonders seen.
I linger beneath the native California Fan Palms,
with a Costa's Hummingbird, a Desert Iguana,
relishing the gift, the grace, of water in the desert.
Is today a metaphor for my life without you?
Hot, dusty, rocky, often hard to find the trail,
savoring the occasional shade or a fleeting breeze?
Will others met along my way and oases yet to be found
make it worth my walking all alone?

Wedding Banquet Triptych

I am truly happy for J and R
because I know how much your love
made my own life worth living.

This is what a fool I am:
surrounded by beautiful women
I wear your ring and dream of you.

Thankfully it is loud pounding music.
Were it *The Twelfth of Never*
I would be in tears knowing
I can never dance with you again.

Grief

How they stare at me in Little Saigon.
Without you I'm just a *haole*
buying chicken feet.

At a picnic table watching the
women at their morning exercise,
their laughter and friendly chatter
in that familiar high pitch
so typical of Vietnamese.
Fresh brewed *Trung Nguyen*,
warm fresh baguette,
real butter and Laughing Cow.
Memories of this same
breakfast with you
in happier times
sweeten my morning.

Mowich! I shout as I drive along,
but there is nobody here now that knows
to look for deer in the meadow.
Our Babel of words and expressions
in English and Cantonese, Klallam and Inupiaq,
Hawaiian, South East Asian tongues and
even the treasured baby-talk of our children,
this private language of ours
that always made us smile with
its lifetime of shared memories,
now has only one native speaker.

The hills were splashed with color
when last we passed this way.
Life with you was so sweet
when cancer was something
that happened to other people
and 'till death do us part
was just a noble sentiment.

Fireflies

Walking in the meadow
of a warm summer eve
my heart sings recalling
your joy and delight
– pure, innocent,
childlike, unbounded –
at delicate lights floating
in the gathering dusk.

Two by two they wink out
until there is just the
dim half-hearted flicker
of a forlorn old has-been
who, consumed by memories
of his lost love and happiness,
lacks the heart to seek a mate
to soften his long, lonely night.

Walking to class I hear the news: JFK shot, classes canceled. Like so many times in our lives when we need to most, we find each other. We spend the afternoon at my apartment listening to the radio and weeping together, connected in our grief to millions of Americans. The president, who inspired us to later join VISTA in answer to the question what can we do for our country, is gone. Watching the impromptu candlelight procession on Telegraph Avenue from the apartment window in the evening, I ask if you want to join them, and despite my sorrow over the day's events my heart leaps knowing the why of your answer No. *We stay in, taking solace in each other's arms until well after eleven when the phone jars us back to reality.* Bring Lainy home! *She's no fool, your Mom, she knows right where to find you. We know the walk to your house by heart, and though scarcely two and a half miles we often take hours to walk it, stopping in the dark to caress, to kiss, to warm icy fingers on bare skin beneath coats and sweaters. I still love you that way, you know, that lips on lips, flesh on flesh, can't get enough of you love. That and countless other ways I learned to love you. Thinking we can get by on nothing but love love, thinking I know you before we are married love and then getting to know you – really getting to know you – love, exploring this big, beautiful world together love, taking Lamaze classes love and being at your side when you give birth love, watching you nurse our babies love, getting up and going to work in the dark while you sleep love, seeing the love you bring to our children love, quitting smoking love, teaching me how a hundred relatives are related without me even realizing it love, quiet time together not needing to talk love, watching you spin, dye, weave, create love, loving the passion you bring to everything you do love, learning there's nothing we can't do if we do it together love, sacrificing our needs for those of our children love, teaching me to appreciate simple pleasures like foo yue and hom yi love, admitting I am wrong love, discovering that our multicultural family is so much richer than the sum of what we two brought to it love, recklessly plunging into life hand in hand without considering the consequences love, learning not to smother you but to let you grow and become who you will love, seeing you repay the anguish that your brother heaps on you with the constant love of a big sister love, doing chores I hate love, loving your stubbornness while protecting you from it love, trusting each other completely love, learning from you to embrace living and never give up love, watching you give Death the fight of his life love, doing everything I can but it is not enough love, helplessly watching you die love, desperately trying to hold on to you while learning to let you go love. November 22. Fifty years of memories of your sweet, sweet life make me smile, make me cry, break my heart and comfort it.*

Lost in sweet memories of
you on other Thanksgivings,
I wonder how we were ever
so young as to think that such
happiness could last forever.

You filled our home with
so much warmth and sunshine
while your cooking filled it
with the heavenly aromas of
lovingly prepared turkey, yams,
homemade cranberry sauce,
apple and pumpkin pies, and
your family's special sticky rice.

I find solace in our kitchen
where I spend my day soaking,
chopping, steaming, chowing,
keeping alive the tradition that
your Dad passed on to you.

Making *now mai fon* for family
is a labor of love, a gift to you
from generations past,
and now your gift to me.

Comfort food for the heart.

Grief

When the kids asked if they could
give me a 70th birthday party
I said *No* because it would just be
too hard to celebrate without you.
But every day is hard without you.
You told me you want me
to live a long and happy life
and I promised I would try,
so why deny myself the
company of those I love?
So I said *Yes*.

It was a lovely day
with our children,
our closest friends,
your favorite cousins,
favorite dishes at Little Hong Kong,
and favorite cake from Hawai'i
enjoyed at your childhood home.

I thought of you all day long
but didn't dare speak of you
lest I fall apart in front of everyone.
Finally at home I just
stood in the kitchen and cried.
Everyone was there for me,
but it was you who filled my heart.

Crying to your picture last night
I told you that no matter how hard
I try to hold on to your memory
I feel you slipping through my fingers.

This morning you were smiling,
lying next to me on our bed
in your comfy wool pants,
favorite purple turtleneck,
dark hair pulled back in a ponytail.
In the midst of the longest,
sweetest kiss in an eternity
came that awful knowledge
that a dream was ending
and I would have to wake.

You always come when I need you most
to reassure me that our love is forever
and to tell me that I should be unafraid
to take another chance on happiness.

Grief

You tried to tell me before you left,
but I couldn't hear through my sorrow.
Because I love you more than life itself
it seems almost a betrayal to have anything
other than a life of despair and grief,
but that is not what you wanted for me.
I must somehow learn to forgive myself
for embracing joy when it comes my way.

You knew me better
than I know myself.
You told me I should
be unafraid to open
my heart to love again.
As always, I was
too stubborn to listen.
Now that my grief
has made itself at home,
settled comfortably into
the landscape of my life,
here I am, as always,
admitting you were right
all along.

Grief

I can't imagine anything more perfect
than this big beautiful blue ball, Earth,
nor a heaven more holy or joyous
than this sweet earthly paradise
that we shared together, my angel.

Tonight
I thank Life for the
blessing of not knowing
what lies on the other side
of Death.

Tonight
if I knew for certain
you were waiting for me,
I would be at your side
in a heartbeat.

Grief

When at last I join you in death
our babies will puzzle at their old man
saving your half-empty perfume bottle.
Will they guess that I was hopelessly
lost in your Chanel No. 5
on the night when first
we dared speak of love?

I finally hear your
whispers in my ear,
telling me that to truly
honor your life and love,
I need to again become
that carefree guy
you fell in love with,
that I need to live my life
with the same joy
and reckless abandon
with which we lived
our life together.

Grief

I never set out to be me.
In my wildest dreams
I never even imagined
becoming this person.
A lifetime of your love
made me who I am,
and now I can't imagine
wanting to be anyone else.

Embracing my grief,
I find that love abides.
Well-meaning friends
want me to move on.
How could they ever think
I would want to get over you?
I choose to continue with my life,
and I choose to take you with me.
Every sorrow, every heartache,
the loneliness and the longing,
even my darkest regrets,
these are just new verses
in the song of our love.

Grief

Soon enough every trace,
every memory of us,
will vanish forever.
For us it was enough
just being together,
alive and in love,
for one glorious lifetime
before returning home
to the bosom of the earth.

No Heaven. No Hell.
All of human folly
gone in a heartbeat.
Only Love remains,
and in Love, you and I,
we are forever.

Grief

I live without you.
You live within me.

www.ingramcontent.com/pod-product-compliance
Lightning Source LLC
Chambersburg PA
CBHW041958080526
44588CB00021B/2796